SECURE FOREVER

Grace Pathway Milestone 2.1

BILL GIOVANNETTI

Endurant Press

© Copyright Bill Giovannetti 2018. All Rights Reserved.

No part of this book may be reproduced or transmitted in any form or by any means, digital, electronic or mechanical, including photocopying, recording, or by an information storage and retrieval system—except by a reviewer who may quote brief passages in a review to be printed in a magazine, newspaper, or on the Web—without permission in writing from the publisher.

Although the author and publisher have made every effort to ensure the accuracy and completeness of information contained in this book, the same assumes no responsibility for errors, inaccuracies, omissions, or any inconsistency herein. Any slights of people, places, or organizations are unintentional. All persons and situations mentioned in this book are fictionalized. Any resemblance to any person, living or dead, is strictly coincidental. Nothing herein shall be construed as a substitute for personal, pastoral, or professional counseling or therapy.

ISBN E-book edition: 978-1-946654-03-8

ISBN Print edition: 978-1-946654-02-1

All scripture quotations, unless otherwise indicated, are taken from the *New King James Version* (R). Copyright © 1982 by Thomas Nelson, Inc. Used by permission. All rights reserved.

Scripture quotations marked (NLT) are taken from the *Holy Bible, New Living Translation,* copyright © 1996, 2004, 2007 by Tyndale House Foundation. Used by permission of Tyndale House Publishers, Inc., Carol Stream, Illinois 60188. All rights reserved.

For additional resources, please visit maxgrace.com.

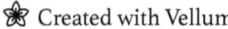 Created with Vellum

ONCE SAVED, ALWAYS SAVED

Neither sin, nor Satan, nor the world can put a Christian out his inheritance. Christ has already taken possession of it in their names and in their stead; and so it is secure to them. If weakness can overcome strength, impotency omnipotency, then may a Christian be kept out of his inheritance – but not until then.

— THOMAS BROOKS, 17TH CENTURY

You can't lose your salvation. Not even if you tried. Not even if you went out and invented a fat, juicy sin nobody has ever done before. Once you're saved you're always saved. That teaching is called Eternal Security, and it is wonderfully scandalous.

This may surprise you. It might even shock you. I hope so, because that means I'm doing my job, which is to preach and teach the kind of good news that goes against everything we naturally expect from God.

If you are saved, you are saved forever.

Once for all.

After all, what good is a salvation that doesn't save in the end? What good is a rescue operation that throws the soggy sinner overboard halfway back to shore? How can *eternal* life be a *temporary* possession?

Does the miracle of new birth come with an off switch?

If the life you have with God can end, can you really call it *eternal*?

The first milestone in the Grace Pathway is that glorious moment when God Saves You. Now, the second milestone is the realization that God Blesses You. Before you earn a single thing, before you serve him, before you change your life, before you do even one good work in the name of Jesus, just because you are saved, God blesses you.

Too bless someone means to give them good gifts that they have not earned and do not deserve.

And the very first of an avalanche of God's blessings in your newly-saved life is his action to secure you in his almighty grip forever.

Let's settle something right here, right now, as you begin your journey with God. You were saved the moment you first believed in Jesus. That salvation "took." It stuck. It sticks forever. Even if you were a kid. Even if you are a backslider. God keeps his word and he's kept it since before you were saved. You were saved, and you will still be saved a million years from now.

Let's find out why.

WHAT IS ETERNAL SECURITY?

Eternal Security means that once you're saved, you're always saved. You cannot lose your salvation. There's nothing you can do, no matter how bad, that will fracture your connection to God.

That's why we use the word *security*. You are secure in your relationship with the Father, the Son, and the Holy Spirit. You are secure in your forgiveness, your adoption into God's "forever family," and in your everlasting life. Like a priceless heirloom, you've been gently placed into God's most secure treasure-house, there to be guarded forever.

Here's a simple definition:

> — ETERNAL SECURITY MEANS THAT
> GOD HIMSELF BEARS ALL THE BURDEN
> TO KEEP YOU SAVED FOREVER.

Your salvation is all of God: from him, by him, and for him. It is all of grace from beginning to end. As the burden was on his shoulders to save you, so it remains on his shoulders to keep you saved.

Not all Christians agree on this teaching. As you go along the Grace Pathway, you will hear some Christian leaders or veteran believers who aren't so sure about whether or not salvation sticks forever. I'm a big fan of being kind-hearted toward those of differing biblical opinion. Those who argue a Christian can lose salvation are not my enemies; this is one of those areas where reasonable Christians disagree.

However, as I read Scripture, I find the evidence for eternal security woven so tightly into the teaching of salvation I just can't see how anyone can separate them.

So here are my top twelve reasons why you can't lose your salvation, resting on four qualities of our God-of-

Almighty-Shoulders: his grace, his power, his faithfulness, and his sovereignty.

Let's go deep!

TIP: As we go along, I will show you a lot of Bible verses. I recommend that you find each one in your Bible, and mark it by highlighting or underlining it in pencil.

SECURED BY THE GRACE OF GOD

The Grace of God is his freely given love, based on everything Jesus did for us when he died and rose again. Here are three reasons why you are secure forever based on the grace of God.

---

1. Because all your sins are fully paid for, even the ones you're going to commit tomorrow.

Jesus, when he died on the Cross, didn't forget a single sin. The specific day when you would actually commit those sins makes no difference. Whether you commit them before you are saved or after doesn't matter. He paid for *all* your sins, past, present, and future. They were all future tense when he died on the cross, and he didn't miss even one of them. He paid in full.

Think about what this means: God would damage his own honor if he were to punish you for a sin Christ already died for. How can that which has been washed away in the flood of Calvary Love ever spoil your salvation?

The Bible says that Jesus, after he had offered the one and only all-sufficient sacrifice to pay for all your sins, "sat down at the right hand of God" (Hebrews 10:12). Why? Because payment for your sins was utterly complete, meaning there is no conceivable circumstance under which you will ever pay for even one of them before God.

- But this Man, after He had offered one sacrifice for sins forever, sat down at the right hand of God. (Hebrews 10:12)
- Therefore there is now no condemnation for those who are in Christ Jesus. (Romans 8:1, NAS95)
- The next day John saw Jesus coming toward him, and said, "Behold! The Lamb of God who takes away the sin of the world!" (John 1:29)
- And He Himself is the propitiation for our sins, and not for ours only but also for the whole world. (1 John 2:2)

---

2. Because your good works weren't required to get you saved, so they can't be required to keep you saved.

When you think about it, there are basically two big reasons why God might conceivably kick you out of his family: too much sin or too little righteousness (goodness, good works). We answered the first reason above, and here's the answer to the second. Good works – including religious observances, morality, and all your human blood, sweat, and tears piled on top of itself and then squared – is completely excluded from the way of salvation.

God saved you, "not by works of righteousness" (Titus 3:5). Paul said, "Therefore by the deeds of the law no flesh will be justified in His sight..." (Romans 3:20). There is no logic or Scripture under which good works can be a condition for continued salvation.

Lewis Sperry Chafer observed, "[A] justification which is not subject to human merit could hardly be subject to human demerit." (Ephesians 2:8,9; Titus 3:5; Zechariah 4:6)

- For by grace you have been saved through faith, and that not of yourselves; it is the gift of God, not of works, lest anyone should boast. (Ephesians 2:8, 9)
- Not by works of righteousness which we have done, but according to His mercy He saved us, through the washing [cleansing power] of regeneration and renewing of the Holy Spirit. (Titus 3:5)
- So he answered and said to me: "This is the word of the LORD to Zerubbabel: 'Not by might nor by power, but by My Spirit,' Says the LORD of hosts. (Zechariah 4:6)
- But to him who does not work but believes on Him who justifies the ungodly, his faith is accounted for righteousness. (Romans 4:5)

---

3. Because, as a Christian, you have been made a full partner in all that belongs to Christ. For God to "unsave" you, he would have to let go of Christ first.

On the day you were saved, something remarkable happened. God joined you to Jesus. He made you one with Christ. You were placed into union with Christ, so that God sees you through Jesus-colored lenses. We will unwrap this wonderful gift in the next book in this series.

For now, it's enough to know this: *Your union with Christ is the ultimate guarantee of your everlasting salvation.* This beautiful gift sets Christianity in a league of its own. God does not bless you directly; he blesses Jesus Christ, and you share his blessings (freely-given gifts). Christ's provision IS your provision. His power IS your power. His holiness IS your holiness. His security IS your security. You have nothing apart from Christ and everything because you are joined to him forever.

Scripture makes the remarkable claim that you have been made equal partners with the Son of God, and are co-included in all his rich blessings forevermore. "And if children, then [you are] heirs – heirs of God and joint heirs with Christ" (Romans 8:17). You did not *earn* this privilege: God, in his marvelous grace, slathered it all over you free of charge.

Therefore, for God to unsave you he would have to either unravel the garment of union with Christ or let Christ fall from his throne. Not in a million eternities. The sparkling streams of amazing grace never will run dry. Never for Jesus, and therefore, never for you either.

- The Spirit Himself bears witness with our spirit that we are children of God, and if children, then heirs--heirs of God and joint heirs with Christ... (Romans 8:16, 17)

- Therefore you are no longer a slave but a son, and if a son, then an heir of God through Christ. (Galatians 4:7)
- There is neither Jew nor Greek, there is neither slave nor free, there is neither male nor female; for you are all one in Christ Jesus. And if you are Christ's, then you are Abraham's seed, and heirs according to the promise. (Galatians 3:28, 29)

SECURED BY THE POWER OF GOD

It's not only the *grace* of God that secures your eternal salvation, it's the *power* of God too. God is all-powerful. The word for this is *omnipotence*. He is infinite in power, and nobody comes close. These next three reasons for eternal security flow out of the omnipotence of God.

---

4. Because your security is now in God's hands, not your own.

In the first moment you trusted Christ, your eternal destiny was eternally taken out of your hands. God took ownership of your future. He wrapped his hand around you, and will never let you go. You are guarded by the omnipotence of God.

He has more power in his little finger than the devil and all the armies of darkness have combined.

With one flex of his bicep, he can silence Satan's accusations, shatter hell's claims, still life's fiercest storms, subdue your heart's darkest passions, snap the chains of the world's allurements, and sweep your life's collected sins into the abyss of Calvary's all-sufficient blood.

God is happily stuck with you. You have no say in the matter.

Let Christ's incredible promise sink deeply into your soul:

- My sheep hear My voice, and I know them, and they follow Me. And I give them eternal life, and they shall never perish; neither shall anyone snatch them out of My hand. My Father, who has given them to Me, is greater than all; and no one is able to snatch them out of My Father's hand. (John 10:27-29)

---

5. Because salvation depends on God's ability, not yours.

All the biblical imagery of God as a shield, strong tower, and defender should squash the thought you can lose your salvation into a little gooey mess. If God is your "strong tower," name one power that's going to break through and drag you out of your saved position. Is he a strong tower or a "strongish" tower?

When the Bible says God "is able," it uses the Greek word *dunameo*, which means "he has the power." God has the power to do what?

Now to Him who is able to keep you from stumbling, And to present you faultless Before the presence of His glory with exceeding joy... (Jude 24)

The same omnipotent arm that spun innumerable stars into orbit, and squeezed mind-numbing energy into every thimbleful of matter — the same Almighty hand that shattered the bars of death to raise Jesus from the tomb — the Lord God Omnipotent himself, has signed in blood an oath to preserve you for his heavenly kingdom. You may fail ten thousand times; but God can do anything but fail.

- And the Lord will deliver me from every evil work and preserve me for His heavenly kingdom. To Him be glory forever and ever. Amen! (2 Timothy 4:18)
- For You have been a shelter for me, A strong tower from the enemy. (Psalms 61:3)
- The name of the LORD is a strong tower; The righteous run to it and are safe. (Proverbs 18:10)
- What then shall we say to these things? If God is for us, who can be against us? (Romans 8:31)

---

6. Because to unsave you, somebody would have to overpower God.

I'm a dad, and I would never let anybody hurt one of my kids. They'd have to kill me first. Your Father in heaven says the same thing.

God adopted you into his family. He became your Father and he takes that role with utmost seriousness. Peter explains that you are "kept" by the power of God forever (1 Peter 1:5). That word, translated "shielded" in some versions, means to post armed guards around someone. That's what God has done for you, only he's the arm and he's the guard.

Who can defeat him? Sin can't. The devil can't. You can't. The demons can't. Your mistakes can't. Your addictions can't. Your rap sheet can't. Your in-laws can't. Your ex- can't. And God won't. Consider yourself secured forever within the invincible arms of God.

- [T]hrough faith [you] are shielded by God's power until the coming of the salvation that is ready to be revealed in the last time. (1 Peter 1:5, NIV)
- Though he fall, he shall not be utterly cast down; For the LORD upholds him with His hand. (Psalm 37:24)
- "Most assuredly, I say to you, he who hears My word and believes in Him who sent Me has everlasting life, and shall not come into judgment, but has passed from death into life. (John 5:24)

SECURED BY THE FAITHFULNESS OF GOD

Not only are you secured by the grace of God and the power of God, you can throw the Faithfulness of God into the mix too. To say God is faithful is to say he is dependable. He never changes, never wavers, and never even flickers. Let's see how the faithfulness of God adds yet another layer to our total security in Christ.

7. Because God promised to save you to the end, and he can't lie.

He is a faithful God – immeasurably more dependable than anyone else in your life. If he promises something, consider it done. If he starts something, consider it finished. When you blow it, he doesn't. When you turn faithless, he remains faithful. Not even the ages of eternity will witness the slightest flicker in the faithfulness of God, and therefore, in his secure grip on you. This is why Paul can say he is "confident of this very thing, that He who has begun a good work in you will complete it until the day of Jesus Christ" (Philippians 1:6).

He.

Will.

Complete.

It.

His faithfulness is great. His mercies are new every single morning without exception forever. With God, there is no shadow of turning, and no variation. He never works in fits and spurts, but like a mighty river, flows on and on in his own character.

For God to reverse your salvation, he would have to be unfaithful to himself, in which case he would cease being God, and this whole created order would have already folded in on itself in a moment of de-creation that would spoil Sunday dinner. Every time I screw up, I thank God he is faithful, and move on. (Titus 1:2. Philippians 1:6. Ecclesiastes 3:14. Hebrews 6:18; 7:24,25; 10:14. 1 Corinthians 1:9. James 1:17)

- In hope of eternal life which God, who cannot lie, promised before time began, (Titus 1:2)
- Being confident of this very thing, that He who has begun a good work in you will complete it until the day of Jesus Christ; (Philippians 1:6)
- I know that whatever God does, It shall be forever. Nothing can be added to it, And nothing taken from it. God does it, that men should fear before Him. (Ecclesiastes 3:14)
- That by two immutable things, in which it is impossible for God to lie, we might have strong consolation, who have fled for refuge to

lay hold of the hope set before us. (Hebrews 6:18)
- But He, because He continues forever, has an unchangeable priesthood. Therefore He is also able to save to the uttermost those who come to God through Him, since He always lives to make intercession for them. (Hebrews 7:24, 25)
- For by one offering He has perfected forever those who are being sanctified. (Hebrews 10:14)
- God is faithful, by whom you were called into the fellowship of His Son, Jesus Christ our Lord. (1 Corinthians 1:9)
- Every good gift and every perfect gift is from above, and comes down from the Father of lights, with whom there is no variation or shadow of turning. (James 1:17)

---

8. Because God won't dump his children.

Most Christians have little clue how enormous the salvation-package is. It's the biggest deal of all the big deals in your life. As part of the deal, God adopted you. You became his child in a special and intimate way. He became to you a loving, ideal Father. Even though you stray, you're still his kid. Even though you're a jerk, he's still your Father. Even though *anything*, he will not kick you out of his family.

God's faithfulness knows no bounds.

In the story of the prodigal son, even though the STD-risking, pierced, lice-ridden, loser of a son was far away from his father's house, he never stopped being his father's son. And so it is with you.

Christ himself issued the iron-clad guarantee that all who come to God by him he "will by no means cast out" (John 6:37). The Greek text uses a strong double negative: he "can't won't" reject you under any circumstance.

- The Spirit Himself bears witness with our spirit that we are children of God, (Romans 8:16)
- Let your conduct be without covetousness; be content with such things as you have. For He Himself has said, "I will never leave you nor forsake you." (Hebrews 13:5)
- "All that the Father gives Me will come to Me, and the one who comes to Me I will by no means cast out." (John 6:37)
- Luke 15:11-32 (The parable of the Prodigal Son)

---

9. Because God won't withdraw his Spirit from you.

Never underestimate the jaw-dropping honor of being the Holy Spirit's home. God is with you and God is for you because God is in you. He has taken up permanent residence within your being. When you got saved, the Holy Spirit moved in.

Paul describes the Spirit's presence as God's downpayment on the full salvation-package. He is the seal on the deal, the ink on the contract, and the earnest of all to come. When it comes to your salvation, there's no going back. Not for you. Not for God. Not for the devil. Not for anyone.

The Father is faithful. The Son is faithful. The Holy Spirit is faithful too. He will never abandon you.

- And you also were included in Christ when you heard the word of truth, the gospel of your salvation. Having believed, you were marked in him with a seal, the promised Holy Spirit, who is a deposit guaranteeing our inheritance until the redemption of those who are God's possession – to the praise of his glory. (Ephesians 1:13, 14, NIV)
- Do you not know that you are the temple of God and that the Spirit of God dwells in you? (1 Corinthians 3:16)
- If we are faithless, He remains faithful; He cannot deny Himself. (2 Timothy 2:13)

SECURED BY THE SOVEREIGNTY OF GOD

Let's remind ourselves of the topic: Eternal Security. God himself bears all the burden to keep you saved forever.

So far, we have looked at three qualities in God's heart that guarantee your salvation: his grace, his power, and his faithfulness.

At this point, you might wonder why we're making the same case in so many ways. The reason is because the world, the devil, and our old pre-saved memories make us doubt God's salvation in so many ways! We must become competent biblical lawyers to make the case against the devil's ceaseless probing of our defenses.

So there is one more quality I'd like us to consider, called God's Sovereignty. This simply means that God is the King. He is the ruling force in the universe. Let's meditate on three more reasons for eternal security that flow out of the Sovereignty of God.

10. Because, once you're saved, your eternal future is already predetermined by God.

There is no getting around the simple truth that once sinners step across the line of faith, their eternal destiny is sealed. It is taken from their control forever. Like strapping into a roller-coaster, they're going for the whole ride because there are no exit ramps.

God has decreed your salvation to last forever, and so it shall.

All the steps leading up to that moment were in his hand, and all the steps leading away from it to the ages of eternity are equally in his hand. Your destiny is so certain that God already calls your future glorification a done deal:

> For whom He foreknew, He also predestined to be conformed to the image of His Son, that He might be the firstborn among many brethren. Moreover whom He predestined, these He also called; whom He called, these He also justified; and whom He justified, these He also glorified. (Romans 8:29,30)

It's a jam-packed verse, but it is saying that your Heavenly King has issued a decree that you will be saved forever. The decree of eternal salvation is eternally unchangeable. This means you can rest your soul in the hands of the sovereign Master and Commander of the Universe. Once he saved you, he sovereignly decreed your salvation would last forever.

No one can ever overrule him.

- Elect according to the foreknowledge of God the Father... (1 Peter 1:2)

- Just as He chose us in Him before the foundation of the world, that we should be holy and without blame before Him in love. (Ephesians 1:4)
- Who shall bring a charge against God's elect? It is God who justifies. (Romans 8:33)
- But we are bound to give thanks to God always for you, brethren beloved by the Lord, because God from the beginning chose you for salvation through sanctification by the Spirit and belief in the truth, to which He called you by our gospel, for the obtaining of the glory of our Lord Jesus Christ. (2 Thessalonians 2:13, 14)

---

11. Because God has willed your salvation to last until the end.

The word "end" in the Bible, means something like a finish line (Greek, *telos*). What's the ultimate finish line for the Christian? Heaven. So Scripture promises this: "[God] will also confirm you to the end [*telos*], that you may be blameless in the day of our Lord Jesus Christ" (1 Corinthians 1:8).

Who will confirm you till the end? You, by your strength? You, by your efforts? Your religion? Your activism? Your moral improvement? No. God alone does this, without one speck of help from you.

He makes you stable and secure in your salvation, doing whatever it takes to keep you saved, until you reach your heavenly finish line.

He will do this in such a way that when the penetrating gaze of the Almighty examines you, you will be found "blameless." Not many people on earth would call you blameless, but God does. This is the power of grace. By it, God has spoken decisively; he will not change his mind.

- For this reason I also suffer these things; nevertheless I am not ashamed, for I know whom I have believed and am persuaded that He is able to keep what I have committed to Him until that Day. (2 Timothy 1:12)
- And the Lord will deliver me from every evil work and preserve me for His heavenly kingdom. To Him be glory forever and ever. Amen! (2 Timothy 4:18)
- [Jesus Christ] will also confirm you to the end, that you may be blameless in the day of our Lord Jesus Christ. God is faithful, by whom you were called into the fellowship of His Son, Jesus Christ our Lord. (1 Corinthians 1:8, 9)
- ...to an inheritance incorruptible and undefiled and that does not fade away, reserved in heaven for you, who are kept by the power of God through faith for salvation ready to be revealed in the last time. (1 Peter 1:4, 5)
- "All that the Father gives Me will come to Me, and the one who comes to Me I will by no means cast out." (John 6:37)

---

12. Because God will overrule any being or power that tries to revoke your salvation.

Try to picture some foolish conspirators forming an elaborate plot to kidnap you from the heavenly realms. They dress in camo, sneak up to heaven's gates, and immediately alarm bells begin to clang. Imagine the lightning bolts of wrath unleashed on them.

Not even Satan can pry you from God's grip. People say that you should hold onto God, and that's good, I guess.

But the real wonder is that he holds onto you. His grip won't slip, and nobody can pry you out of his hand. No, not even you yourself on your very worst day.

- For I am persuaded that neither death nor life, nor angels nor principalities nor powers, nor things present nor things to come, nor height nor depth, nor any other created thing, shall be able to separate us from the love of God which is in Christ Jesus our Lord. (Romans 8:38,39)

SERIOUSLY SAVED

The overwhelming testimony of Scripture is this: God himself bears all the burden to get you saved, keep you saved, and bring you safely home at last. In the chain that connects you to heaven, not one link has been forged by your own might. Otherwise, you'd be doomed – for the whole chain would only be as strong as its weakest link.

But in grace, God has set all your works aside. Salvation stands forever as his work, beginning, middle, and end.

- God is gracious, and therefore, you are secure forever.
- God is omnipotent, and therefore, you are secure forever.
- God is faithful, and therefore, you are secure forever.
- God is sovereign, and therefore, you are secure forever.

What more could you ask for?

A little voice inside might hiss, "It's too good to be true." And that is exactly how grace always sounds.

That little voice in your head, making you fret over your salvation, needs to shut up.

That little voice in your head, convincing you to cower and grovel before your Maker, is telling you a lie.

That little voice in your head, driving you to pray for salvation over and over again, is spouting the doctrines of demons; don't be a sucker.

Once saved, always saved.

That's how effective the death and resurrection of Christ is.

HIS INTEGRITY AT STAKE

There's an old preacher's story about a little old lady on her deathbed. Her novice pastor came to visit to make sure she was ready to go.

"Don't worry about me," she said, eyes gleaming, and voice warbling. "I know the Lord is mine and I am his."

Her preacher gasped. Having been reared by a pack of howling legalists, he had no room in his theology for such breathtaking confidence. He tried to talk some humility into her.

"Yes, but, God must judge you according to your deeds, and 'be sure your sins will find you out,' and..."

She shushed him.

"Young man," she said, "If I don't go to heaven when I die, then God will lose far more than I will lose."

The pastor sputtered with indignation. "What? Do you realize how arrogant..."

She interrupted him. "Listen. If I don't go to heaven, I

will lose my soul forever, that is all. But, if I don't go to heaven, God will lose his integrity. For he has promised to take to heaven all those who come to him by Christ, and that is how I have come."

Can I get an amen?

Does this mean you can go out tomorrow and commit a sin and still go to heaven? The lawyer I sleep with (my wife) is very concerned about this rhetorical question; she wants me to issue all kinds of caveats and warnings, but I won't. I will simply let grace stand there naked, and scandalous, and without qualifiers.

The answer is yes, with no buts in sight. Even if you could invent a new sin, you would never lose your salvation. It just doesn't depend on you. It all depends on Christ.

Whatever consequences for sin there may be in a Christian's life, you will never find dismissal from God's family among them.

A JOURNEY ON SOLID FOOTING

The Grace Pathway is a journey on solid footing. It's a path you're happily stuck on.

You can't take yourself away from God. The devil can't take you away from God. Your pastor, priest, or pope can't take you away from God. God won't take you away from God. So what can separate you from God? Absolutely nothing.

You might feel shaky.

You might feel insecure and weak.

Regardless of feelings, the fact is you are secure forever in the hands of your Father. Calvary Love is all the guarantee you need.

If you were saved at the beginning of this year, you'll still be saved at the end of it. And a decade from now and a century from now, you'll still be saved. And when the mountains crumble into the sea, and this old earth begins to dissolve, and our sun burns out its fuel and eternity rolls on, forever and evermore, you will still find yourself gripped by the grace and power of a God who loved you and gave himself for you.

> *The soul that on Jesus hath lean'd for repose.*
> *I will not, I will not desert to his foes;*
> *That soul, though all hell should endeavor to shake,*
> *I'll never, no never, no never forsake.*

— AUTHOR UNKNOWN, 1700S

YOU CAN BE SURE

Uncertainty as to our relationship with God is one of the most enfeebling and dispiriting of things. It makes a man heartless. It takes the pith out of him. He cannot fight; he cannot run. He is easily dismayed and gives way. He can do nothing for God. But when we know that we are of God, we are vigorous, brave, invincible. There is no more quickening truth than this of Assurance.

— HORATIUS BONAR, 1800S

Hi, my name is Bill. I know I am going to heaven. I know my sins are forgiven. I know God loves me and lives inside me, and I am his child. I know these things, not because I am a better person than anybody else, not because I am a pastor – paid to be holy – and not because I am a charmingly good-looking Italian.

I know these things because the Bible tells me so, and I have the priceless commodity known in theology as *Assurance*.

Assurance is the flip side of eternal security's coin.

Eternal security is the Christian's objective reality; Assurance is the Christian's subjective confidence.

Scripture is clear: eternal life is not a "hope so" proposition; it is a "know so" proposition:

> These things I have written to you who believe in the name of the Son of God, that you may know that you have eternal life, and that you may continue to believe in the name of the Son of God. (1 John 5:13)

I am not keeping my fingers crossed and hoping for the best. I am resting in the finished work of Jesus Christ as my only hope, and if that's not enough, I've got no Plan B. The biggest question of my life has been answered: I will spend eternity with God. No nagging doubts, no hellfire fears, and no heavenly frown threatens my peace with God. Though I am deeply conscious – and ever increasingly so – of my innate unworthiness, I am gripped by a hand of grace that I know will never let me go.

It wasn't always this way for me. Though I had been saved as a kid, I was freaked out that it didn't stick. The buckshot of legalism punctured a thousand holes in my confidence. One phrase in particular worried me – it came from my Sunday School teacher more times than I could count. He would describe something good that Christians should be doing, and then lean in to say, "If you're not doing [insert radical-type duty here], you'd better check your salvation experience!"

But I had a huge problem: having been saved very young, I couldn't remember my salvation experience. There was no experience for me to check. So I did what any self-respecting eight, nine, or ten year old would do: I prayed to receive Christ again. And again and again and again. I begged. I pleaded. I promised to try harder.

My doubts were not born of humility; they were the oozing scabs of Grace Deficit Disorder.

I knew the gospel outline, but it was so inconsistently intermingled with behavioral obligations, I never felt I'd done enough.

That anxiety slimed me like toxic mold. I prayed, read my Bible, shared my faith, knocked on doors to witness to strangers (oh, the humanity), played in my church worship band, never missed a prayer meeting, helped in Awana clubs, and helped with the youth group. All of this as a teenager.

Much of this stemmed from an unresolved anxiety over God.

When I was seventeen, God flipped a switch for me, and dropped the gift of assurance in my lap with such force I've never looked back.

I was sitting in my cavernous high school gym in urban Chicago on a day when my gym teacher was absent. We were told to sit in the stands and do homework. I read a book. What I read blew my guilt-ridden, anxiety-induced, fear-driven, God-avoidant, damnation-brooding fretfulness out of the window once for all.

How?

By reading the first explanation of the Cross of Christ that really clicked for me.

Suddenly, God converted an echo-filled, stale gymnasium into a sanctuary. The noise of pick-up basketball slipped into the background and my eyes were opened to the finality of the Cross. In that moment, I knew I was saved. I knew my sins were gone. A weight had been lifted off my shoulders.

It wasn't the day of my salvation; I was quite conscious of that. It was the day of my assurance.

Christ really did pay my debt in full.

Christ really did die for me.

God really did love me.

I really could come to him "just as I am."

I really was saved.

It really did stick the hour I first believed.

I really was a beloved member of the family of God all because of my Savior's blood.

I felt no pride, no presumption. Just a burden rolled away and a hope given wings. I have never seriously doubted my salvation since that day.

I've thought long and hard, over the years, wondering what made the difference. The truths I read that day were nothing new. I'd heard them in bits and pieces all my life. But something clicked for me. What was it? What was the secret of my assurance?

THE WORD OF GOD

I know beyond all doubt I am saved forever because the Bible tells me so. Jesus promised whoever comes to God by him he will "by no means cast out" (John 6:37). I have come to God by him.

Christ's language is emphatic – a double negative, like a one-two punch in legalism's face. He will not hurl you out of his affections. He will not hurl you out of his arms. He will not hurl you out of his family. He will not hurl you out of the justification, redemption, propitiation, or salvation in which you stand. He will not hurl you out of his glorious, blood-bought church.

He promised.

What more proof do you need?

The title-deed to your mansion in heaven has been signed in blood, sealed by the Spirit, and given to you in writing.

God invites you to come near "with a true heart in full assurance of faith" (Hebrews 10:22). This is the assurance birthed by Scripture integrated into your soul.

Paul prays for Christians to attain "to all the riches of the full assurance of understanding" (Colossians 2:2). This is the breathtaking confidence bubbling up from ever-deepening scriptural wells of grace in Jesus Christ.

The author of Hebrews desires that Christians "show the same diligence to the full assurance of hope until the end" (Hebrews 6:11). A promise from a God who cannot lie has got to be the surest bet in life and death.

When God invites you to "come boldly to the throne of grace," he presumes a certain level of assurance (Hebrews 4:16). To step boldly before God? Really? That is nothing but a giant round peg in the painfully tiny square hole of all your doubts and fears.

In the early days of Christianity, three thousand people were saved on one day. They were immediately added to the church and were baptized (Acts 2:41). Why the rush? Why not wait for fruit to develop? After all, shouldn't church leaders wave their good-works detectors over new converts' lives for a while to see if any holiness registers? Wouldn't that make more sense?

No.

Because salvation is as certain in that first hour as it will be in the ages of eternity. It is as certain for the Christian as the love of the Father is for the Son.

It is an immutable promise from an immutable God to a people he knows are embarrassingly mutable, so he draws a line, invites them to cross it, and scoops them into his forever family the moment they do.

On your worst day, if you can scrape together the faith to do it, you can show the divine contract to the heavenly Covenanter and insist he fulfill his end of the bargain.

And he will.

He loves that kind of audacious faith.

In fact, he'll fulfill his covenant whether you ask him to or not. Because God accomplishes his will on days when you don't care. What he promises he does. What he starts he finishes. You are not the point. Sorry. His own integrity is the point.

> *Jesus loves me, this I know,*
> *For the Bible tells me so.*

What more proof do I need?

None.

God gives the grace of assurance to all who will receive it. Like any blessing of grace, it is offered freely, as part of salvation's inheritance, to anyone who takes God at his Word. Assurance is offered to you, if you'll have it.

Faith.

I don't know your heart; that's between you and God.

I don't know what you've believed or not believed, received or not received. The early church baptized men and women upon their *profession* of faith; evidence would come later.

It isn't for me or you to judge.

What is for us is the abiding promise of God:

He who has the Son has life; he who does not have the Son of God does not have life. (1 John 5:12)

What an incredible promise! What a great salvation! Before you go out and serve God or get busy for Jesus, anchor your heart in this wonderful truth: God himself bears ALL the burden to keep you saved forever. Before you ever do one thing for God, take your stand on the solid ground that God blesses you better than you'll ever know.

Welcome to God's Everlasting, Never-Shrinking, Forever-Blessed Family!

WHAT'S NEXT

Keep going! There are more awesome discoveries ahead! Here are all the booklets in the Grace Pathway Series.

Milestone 1/ God Saves You (Live!)
1.0 — Welcome to God's Family

Milestone 2/God Blesses You (Obtain!)
2.1 — Secure Forever <<<—*YOU ARE HERE*
2.2 — You're Richer Than You Think
2.3 — How to Have a Quiet Time

Milestone 3/ God Grows You (Mature!)
3.1 — Knowing God
3.2 — The Cross
3.3 — The Basics

Milestone 4/ God Uses You (Activate!)
4.1 Understanding Your Spiritual Gifts
4.2 How to Share Your Faith
4.3 Know Why You Believe (Apologetics)

All of these booklets are available on Amazon, Barnes and Noble, and wherever books are sold. You can order bulk copies and customized copies for your church at www.maxgrace.com.

www.ingramcontent.com/pod-product-compliance
Lightning Source LLC
Chambersburg PA
CBHW052210110526
44591CB00012B/2151